DEVOTIONS FOR YOUNG PEOPLE

GOOD MORNING, LORD

**Devotions for
Young People**

Paul Martin

BAKER BOOK HOUSE
Grand Rapids, Michigan

Scripture quotations other than from the King James version are as
follows:

*The New Testament: Today's English Version (Good News for Modern
Man).* Copyright 1966 by the American Bible Society, New York.

Revised Standard Version of the Holy Bible. Copyright 1946, 1952 by
the Division of Christian Education of the National Council of
Churches.

The New Testament in Modern English. Copyright © by J. B. Phillips,
1958. Used by permission of the Macmillan Company.

IN APPRECIATION

I have been grateful for the response to the *Good Morning Lord* series. Many incidents of those who gained strength and encouragement from reading the books have come to me.

So may this one ... in its light pages and dark ... in its laughter and prayer ... bring cheer, and hope to all.

I have a son and daughter-in-law, who are a source of inspiration and joy. To them, Michael and Gloria, I dedicate this book of rambling thoughts ... in the prayer that their hands and lives will give much more to their day.

—Paul Martin

FOREWORD

Another book from Paul Martin! Just as fresh, just as vital, and just as contagious as the others he has written!

Devotions for Young People reflects the personality of the author. This is the way he lives, preaches, and witnesses. Good humor, optimism, and practical religion are basic ingredients in his life and ministry.

This book is written primarily for young people. But I suspect that older folk will read it with the same zest and relish as the young. It's a practical book. Brief, pungent thoughts for each day that penetrate and grip and lift.

Here's a man who is still youthful in spirit and blest by the Spirit after thousands of miles and thousands of churches in his evangelistic labors. Here's a book with freshness, vibrancy, and challenge to make each day a good day in God's presence.

This book was written to be read. To be read daily. Those who do will "have a good day."

—George Coulter
General Superintendent
Church of the Nazarene

A day in thy courts is better than a thousand.
—Ps. 84:10

HAVE A GOOD DAY!

And why not! God lives. God loves. God cares. A day with Him is worth a thousand.

Life is full of days. They come and go.... I cannot stop them. So let's have a good day!

Whether or not it is a good day depends on where you spend it. Let's have a good day, then, in His presence. "In the courts of the Lord."

In His presence ... it is peaceful. His courts are "amiable," friendly. His words are good to hear.

In His presence ... it is joyful. His courts ring with laughter and song.

In His presence ... is healing and comfort and understanding. Where He is ... it is love alive.

So enter His presence with expectation. Come into His courts with praise.

For a day in His presence is worth a thousand days of loneliness and fear.

Have a good day!

PRAYER FOR TODAY:

Dear God, I have today.... It is here.... Make it a good day for me ... and, through me, to others.

But this one thing I do, forgetting those
things which are behind, and reaching forth
unto those things which are before, I press [on].
—Phil. 3:13-14

YESTERDAY—LONG GONE

I may have failed, and fallen flat . . . but that is yesterday. I have today to do better, to fix the damage I did when I fell, and then go on.

I may have argued, debated, and pulled hard with a loved one or a friend. But that is yesterday. I have today to reflect, to show understanding . . . to care.

I may have shown prejudice and fear . . . when the heat was on . . . but that is yesterday. I have today . . . to say "I'm sorry" . . . and show courage.

I may have been too hilarious . . . and have driven roughly through the quiet lives of others. But that is yesterday. I have today to stop dead still for a moment . . . and then get at the job again.

I cannot go back to yesterday but I will want to remember its lessons . . . for I must not learn those lessons again. Yesterday is gone. I will not let it haunt me nor will I let it go unheeded.

So, remembering the lessons of yesterday and forgetting its failures, let's face today!

REMEMBER THIS:

> *The world is wide*
> *In time and tide*
> *And God is Guide.*
> *Don't hurry.*

*Take therefore no thought for the morrow: for the
morrow shall take thought for the things of itself.
Sufficient unto the day is the evil thereof.*
—Matt. 6:34

*HAVE A GOOD DAY—
TOMORROW IS NOT HERE*

Borrowing may be necessary. But one of the hardest things in
the world to do is to make "ten easy payments."

But the most foolish borrowing is to borrow from tomorrow!
Here are some lyrics for my new song (you write the music):

> Don't borrow from tomorrow
> It may never come.
> It is enough to live this day
> And get its hard work done.
> Don't borrow from tomorrow,
> We'll need its joys in time.
> Enjoy today, its work, its play,
> And do your best . . . (Put in a word that
> rhymes with "time," thanks.)
> Don't borrow from tomorrow,
> We have just today,
> And God has grace for every task,
> Along this happy way.

(The music for this new song should be easy to sing, with a
sparkling beat, and close harmony. And I don't suggest an oboe
or a tuba for accompaniment!)

A SONG TO SING: (I mean a real song)

> *All the way my Savior leads me.
> What have I to ask beside?
> Can I doubt His tender mercy
> Who through life has been my guide?*
> —Fanny J. Crosby

9

*As a father pitieth his children, so
the Lord pitieth them that fear him.*
—Ps. 103:13

WE ARE JUST PEOPLE

Not animals, not here by chance
We are people, God's people.
Some are fat, some are thin,
Some are long, some are short,
Some are easy to look at, some are not.

We are so different. It is hard to realize we have the same Father.

God is our Father. He really is a father . . . in understanding, in love, in care. The word *pitieth* means "shows compassion, loves to fondle, gives mercy." God does this. He is a good Father.

His goodness is shown in these ways:

1. He has plans for you. He has some good things going for you. There is purpose, direction, and meaning in His plans. Life is not a dead end to God. He knows the way through the wilderness. . . . Let's follow!

2. God's plan is to give us a good life. No, not an easy life . . . but satisfying. No, not always dead sure and never discouraged . . . but confident and trusting.

3. He provides the strength and the wisdom to take His way! He does not just talk about it; He gave Jesus, our Savior; He gave the Holy Spirit, our Sanctifier and Guide. He gives, and gives, and gives, and gives again.

A LITTLE VERSE FOR TODAY:

*So I go on not knowing,
 I would not if I might;
I would rather walk in the dark with God
 Than go alone in the light.*

—Mary Brainard

10

When I consider thy heavens, the work of thy
fingers, the moon and the stars, which thou hast
ordained; what is man, that thou art mindful of him? and
the son of man, that thou visitest him?
—Ps. 8:3-4

WHAT COLOR IS GOD?

Yes, we have the same Father. But what color is He? Where is He? What is He doing?

There are some great mysteries about God! He is above our understanding! He is bigger than I can imagine, yet small enough to be personal with me! I bow before Him . . . great God of all things. . . . yet my personal Friend.

Buzz Aldrin read the verse above from his space ship to a world television audience as he sped home from "moon-walking." He had a great God in mind.

What color is God? The same as you! You are made in His image. He is the maker of colors. In Him all colors are mixed . . . are one.

Where is He? He's where you are. He is where I am. Really, the right question is . . . Where are you? You are in the presence of God. "He is here and He is there and all the way between."

What is God doing? You'll never really know all He is doing! He is the "Beginner" and is still creating. He is the "Finisher" and is completing what He started. He is the Maker of man. And this caused some problems, for He gave man reason, imagination, emotion, and the power to choose. Now God is in love with His man! He is rescuing, healing, forgiving, and leading those who will let Him. He is mighty busy!

A GOOD MAN SAID THIS:

"There comes a time when we have to believe what we cannot prove, and to accept where we cannot understand."
—William Barclay

11

Rest in the Lord, and wait patiently for him.
—Ps. 37:7

BACK TO SLEEP

The alarm-radio came booming on.

"Any more requests?"

"Have you any back-to-sleep music? I'm out, really out."

"How about a Schubert quartette; or how about 'Gymnopedies, One and Two,' by Erik Satie; or a few choice hits of 'Atom Heart Mother,' with Pink Floyd?"

"How can I have a good day when I can't wake up."

W. D. McGraw tells about a chap who on Monday would send his wife out early for the newspaper and first check the obituaries. If his name wasn't listed, he knew he was alive and he'd get going Tuesday.

Maybe you are a "p.m. person" . . . alive at night, and pretty hazy in the a.m. Or if you are embarrassed about last night or what's coming today, it is hard to have a good day. The Lord can help in these things. Ask Him.

You can ask His patience and forgiveness for yesterday . . . you can talk about today's fears with Him ahead of time . . . and get up and go.

If you are just tired, have a good sleep and get at it now. The day can start when you are ready.

A HYMN-LINE FOR TODAY:

> *Open my eyes, that I may see*
> *Glimpses of truth Thou hast for me.*
> —Charles H. Scott

12

Greet Priscilla and Aquila my helpers
in Christ Jesus: . . . Likewise greet
the church that is in their house.
—Rom. 16:3-5

WHAT IS THE CHURCH?

Is it a building? Of course it is. It is a tent, a clearing in the woods, or a house. It is where God and people get together! It is a house of prayer.

But what is the church? Is it just a building? Of course not; it is never just a place. The church is people. "Not a fold but a flock . . . not a sacred building . . . but a believing assembly." Someone said, "Clothes do not make a man," nor do bricks and stone make a church.

So the church members are friends of Christ . . . who usually get together in some place for encouragement. . . . That's what is called the church.

And the church is a life-saving station. At its altars many are finding peace and eternal life. And the church goes out. It does not wait for the sin-sick to come. The church goes out and brings the Savior to them.

So the church is all this and more. What is the church to you?

MR. ANONYMOUS WROTE THIS:

And whether it be a rich church, or a poor church, anywhere;
Truly it is a great church if God is worshiped there.

*All scripture is given by inspiration of God,
and is profitable for doctrine, for reproof, for
correction, for instruction in righteousness.*
—II Tim. 3:16

PLACED BY THE GIDEONS

It is as common as the TV in the room, as attractive as the lamp, available, ready ... in hotels, motels, hospitals, some schools, and in the hands of many servicemen ... the Gideon Bible!

There are three things that make it great:

1. It is truly the Bible, God's word. It gives comfort in time of sorrow, relief in time of suffering, guidance in time of decision, courage in time of fear, peace in time of turmoil, strength in time of temptation, warning in time of indifference. It is God talking to man.

2. The Gideon Bible is great ... for it is there! Truly available. You never have to look for it. Placed right where you are. In the copy I am holding right now, there is a section which says: "There is a verse in the Bible which has been translated into over 1,100 languages. It tells of One who loved us with an everlasting love. And here is that verse in 25 languages which are understood by three-fourths of the world's population, John 3:16." And there they are: Afrikaans, Arabic, Chinese, Danish, Dutch, English, Finnish, French, German, Greek, Hindu, Hebrew, Icelandic, Italian, Japanese, Korean, Malay, Norwegian, Portuguese, Russian, Sinhalese, Spanish, Swedish, Tamil, and Vietnamese! For all to read and be saved!

3. The Gideon Bible is a love story. . . . It is provided by men filled with God's love ... who have given of their time and their means for this cause for over seventy-five years.

QUOTE FOR TODAY:

*"The testimony of the Lord is sure, making wise the simple"
(Ps. 19:7).*

14

I had rather be a doorkeeper in the house
of my God, than to dwell in the tents of wickedness.
—Ps. 84:10

AT THE FRONT DOOR

"Even the threshold of His presence is better than to be 'in' with the crowd." This is especially for you ... you who are just coming into His presence.

You may not believe it ... but God takes notice of all who start His way.

And it is so much better, isn't it, to start ... just start His way? ... The coming is toward God.... This is so much better than going with the group.

At the front door of His presence is just the beginning ... with so much out there ... a mansion to explore, a big house to investigate.

Inside the "tents" it is perishable, passing ... so very temporary. No place that satisfies ... easily blown away. These are the tents of wickedness. This is the life of selfishness.

Though inside, they seem unsuccessful and accomplished. Still it is a tent.

One has translated the above verse: "I would choose rather to sit at the threshold of the Lord's presence than to dwell in the tents of the wicked." Wouldn't you?

A HYMN-LINE FOR TODAY:

Change and decay in all around, I see;
O Thou who changest not, abide with me."
—Henry F. Lyte

Don't let the world around you squeeze you into its own
mold, but let God remold your minds from within, so that you may
prove in practice that the plan of God for you is good, meets
all his demands and moves toward the goal of true maturity.
—Rom. 12:2 (Phillips)

A TIGHT SQUEEZE

There are three good reasons why others around would press you into their mold:

1. A strong, faithful stand for God and right makes others uncomfortable. For all have sinned and most of us know where and when. It troubles weak, compromising souls to see a clear, definite witness.

2. It is easier to beg, cajole, or entice someone to drift like the rest than to turn about and start a good fight. I have often thought that if these squeezers would just use the same energy to get going for God that they use to try to get *you* to join *them* . . . they would be saints for sure!

3. The devil helps those who coast along. He is really pressing for all to join the "broad way" that leads away from God. He uses all his power and wit.

The scripture verse for today says plainly that we must let God remold our minds, capture our wills. We are no match for these squeezers. But God will cleanse our minds . . . fortify our wills. He'll do a miracle of love within that will prove His way is the right way.

A SING-ALONG FOR TODAY:

> *I'm pressing on the upward way.*
> *New heights I'm gaining every day;*
> *Still praying as I onward bound,*
> *"Lord, plant my feet on higher ground."*
> —Johnson Oatman, Jr.

*I am come that they might have life, and
that they might have it more abundantly.*
—John 10:10

LIFE

I was right in the middle of them, 1,600 high school kids, some singing, some in the good, loud band. It was "Life," a musical message to young hearts.

It was Estes Park, Colorado, 1970. The music overpowered me.

> You can have Life if you want it.
> You can have Life this very day.
> You can have a brand-new way of living.
> You can have Life.
> It is contagious. It is being born again.
> Don't be a phony. A phony never wins.
>
> What will other people think?
>
> Try it. You have the power to choose.
> He is the Way, He is the Truth, He is the Life.
>
> There's a bright new Life that's so exciting
>   And you can have this Life if you decide.
> The Lord can fill that lonely, empty feeling.
>   He'll give you joy and happiness inside.*

How the Spirit worked! A compelling feeling gripped us.

When they started to sing, "Right now, commit your life, right now," I urged the convicted ones to come to the front or stand where they were. Scores came and prayed.

All right, I'm excited. But it is the truth. You can have Life if you want it, right now.

A PROMISE THAT IS AS REAL AS JESUS:

"If we confess our sins, he is faithful and just to forgive us our sins, and to cleanse us from all unrighteousness."

—I John 1:9

*Otis Skillings, "Life," © 1971 by Lillenas Pub. Co.
    All rights reserved.

17

He had compassion on him, and went
to him, . . . and took care of him.
—Luke 10:33-34

THE SURPRISING SAMARITAN

A lawyer asked Jesus, "Who is my neighbour?"

The story Jesus told is full of surprises. . . . A surprising answer to a surprising question.

A traveler from Jerusalem to Jericho is surprised by thieves who rob him, beat him, and leave him half dead. Two professional religious men, a priest and a Levite, pass the sufferer by . . . acting in a surprising way. (Too busy being religious to be compassionate.)

And the Samaritan comes to the hurt one's rescue . . . quite a surprise! He has heart!

He acts in a surprising manner: He does not panic, he does not faint.

He does not blunder. "A warm heart makes a cool head." Look what he does: He washes the wounds, lifts the sufferer to his beast, guides the animal carefully over the rocks, brings the victim to the inn, cares for him through the night. In the morning, he quietly pays the bill in advance so there will be no embarrassment.

Who is my neighbor? It is anyone . . . right down the road.

A PRAYER:

Dear Lord, I know I have neighbors. Help me go to them, with You. I can't save the whole world but I can act like You with my neighbors.

18

And the Lord spake unto Moses face to
face, as a man speaketh unto his friend.
—Exod. 33:11

JUST JESUS AND YOU

Did you ever have a song keep going over and over in your
head . . . or somewhere?

Yesterday and today this gospel chorus has been "bugging"
me:

> Now it is Jesus and me, for each tomorrow,
> For ev'ry heartache, and ev'ry sorrow.
> I know that I can depend upon my newfound Friend,
> And so to the end, it's Jesus and me.*

We need a real friend, you and I.

Those who study such things say that if one who is tempted
to commit suicide can find just one good friend with whom he
can be himself . . . talk it out, and know he is wanted and
needed, . . . the chances of suicide are lessened.

Add to this that Jesus, our Savior, will be a real Friend . . . if
we let Him!

For even though He knows the worst about us, He forgives.
He is always available, ready, close. He shows us where we are
needed. His words are just what we must have!

AN OLD SAYING TO TAKE WITH YOU TODAY:

> *And though this world with devils filled,*
> *Should threaten to undo us.*
> *We will not fear, for God hath willed*
> *His truth to triumph through us.*
>
> —Martin Luther

*Ira Stanphill. Copyright, 1946, Singspiration, Inc.

19

*For if you forgive others the wrongs they have done
you, your Father in heaven will forgive you.*
—Matt. 6:14 (*Today's English Version*)

FORGIVENESS

Can we estimate the power or the scope of one word?

Forgiveness: It brings light to the dark past. It is deeper than the deepest sea. It conveys the greatest experience in all the world!

Forgiveness: It is of God. It cost God His very best, Jesus Christ. Begone, guilt! Begone, misery! God forgives.

Forgiveness: A way of life for Jesus. "Father, forgive them, for they know not what they do." "Neither do I condemn thee: go, and sin no more."

Forgiveness: The way of good living at home. Parents feel better when they practice it. Children grow stronger as they learn it!

Forgiveness is the enemy of pride. Pride is of the heart of sin. A forgiving spirit defeats the devil.

Forgiveness is the language of heaven. We'll need it to get there. We'll have to forgive others to enjoy heaven.

Oh, I wish, *somehow,* that forgiveness would circle the whole world . . . that war would cease . . . that killing would be done away . . . that man would live with man in peace.

PRAYER FOR TODAY:

"Forgive us what we owe You, as we forgive what others owe us!"

"What about you?" He asked them. *"Who do you say I am?"*
—Matt. 16:15 (*Today's English Version*)

WHAT ABOUT JESUS?

Do you know what we did, one day, in Phoenix, Arizona? A young man and I went from house to house asking this question. "What do you think of Jesus Christ?" We got a lot of answers, but no one asked back, "Who is He?" nor did anyone say, "Never heard of Him; guess we should have had our TV fixed."

Who is He? What does Jesus mean to you?

To those who are wondering, misled . . . He is the Way! His way is challenging . . . upstream against the easy flow of selfishness and sin.

To the emptyhearted, the "naked in heart" . . . He is a Robe of truth and understanding.

To the hungry who search for meaning, for sense, for purpose . . . He is the Bread.

To the sin-sick, the dying, the weary . . . He is the Great Physician.

To the dead in trespasses and sin . . . He is Life, real Life!

To the poor in spirit, poor in life . . . He is the Giver of riches: a clear conscience, a life of meaning, and heaven too.

What is He to you?

A GOOD WORD FROM A GOOD MAN:

> *Without the Way, thou canst not go,*
> *Without the Truth, thou canst not know,*
> *Without the Life, thou canst not live.*
>
> —Thomas A Kempis

Men that have hazarded their lives for
the name of our Lord Jesus Christ.
—Acts 15:26

IT IS NOT TOO HARD—FOR US

Having it pretty hard? The preacher spoke to you about some idle words!

Pretty difficult, is it? . . . trying to pay your tithe and make payments on your television?

Uphill, all the way, is it? Learning to witness in a noisy world?

A lot of people at school tease you about being a Christian, do they? Even call you "Preach."

Not too easy to be a Christian . . . temptations strong . . . the devil relentless? Yes.

But God does not promise ease. God does not promise a life without struggle, without pain, without death.

Look what happened to the first disciples and breathe a thankful sigh you are a Christian today.

James, brother of Jesus, and Stephen, the first martyr, are killed by the mobs in Jerusalem; Matthew is slain with a sword in Ethiopia; Philip is hanged in Phrygia; Bartholomew is whipped to death in Armenia; Andrew is crucified in Achaia; Thomas is run through with a lance in East India; Thaddeus is shot to death with arrows; Simon the Zealot dies on a cross in Persia; and Peter dies upside down on a cross in Rome; Matthias is beheaded; James the son of Zebedee, killed with a sword on orders from Herod. Only John escapes, although boiled in oil, and is banished to Patmos.

Feel better?

SING AGAIN:

> *Faith of our fathers! holy faith!*
> *We will be true to thee till death!*
> (Sing all of it.)

22

For I know nothing by myself
. . . but
he that judgeth me is the Lord.
—I Cor. 4:4

A DOG ON THE BASES

Dave Baker, former professional football player and athletic director now at a Christian college, tells this story:

"In Kansas City, Missouri, last summer, a dog ran onto the baseball field. Dogs do that. They like ball games. The game was stopped. Ole Bouser touched first base, ran to second, and beat it to third. There he sat, triumphantly! The crowd was hilarious. Over the crowd, some suggestions could be heard:

> Bite the umpire!
> Head for home!
> Go back where you came from!
> Go get your bone!
> Play shortstop!

A sportswriter commenting on the scene said, "Really, the only thing of importance here is that there was not a dominant voice in the crowd that could give directions!"

So we run the bases today . . . just run . . . in circles.

What a day for a voice of certainty . . . a strong witness for Jesus the Way. You can be that witness. Be definite, positive, with a smile for God. He is the Answer people are looking for.

A GOOD QUOTE TODAY:

"For these times faith must have fiber and force; it must have roots knotted on great convictions and muscles applied to great tasks."

—T. Crichton Mitchell

How much then is a man better than a sheep?
—Matt 12:12

NOBODY—GOING NOWHERE

Consider the problem of the air-freight clerk. A dog was being shipped by air but somewhere and somehow the shipping slip and tag on the box were lost. There was no way to tell who was the dog's owner or where he was going or where he came from. The clerk decided to send the dog to the airline's lost-and-found department and put this tag on the crate: "Name: Nobody; destination: nowhere; from: no one."

That's the tag many of us carry. We are not sure who we are, where we are going, or what we shall do.

This may seem too simple an answer for you but it's my answer.

Who am I? A friend of God. A life . . . my being is a creation of God. My power to choose is a gift of God. Since I am part of God's creation, I am set upon by the devil. He is an enemy of God, a destroyer.

What am I doing? Given a good chance, I am to live unselfishly, share the fruits of life with others, reach out to those in bondage as others reached out to me.

Where am I going? Life is eternal. I am going toward a bigger life, a life free of binding restraints. Death comes. It is change, a startling change. But love will triumph in death.

So I am someone, a friend of God; going somewhere in His presence; doing something to lift, to ease, to brighten another's journey in a dark time.

A GOOD SONG FOR THIS MOMENT:

> *In simple trust, like those who heard*
> *Besides the Syrian sea*
> *The gracious calling of the Lord,*
> *Let us, like them, without a word,*
> *Rise up and follow Thee.*
>
> —Frederick C. Maker

*This is a true saying, to be completely accepted
and believed: Christ Jesus came into the world
to save sinners. I am the worst of them.*
—I Tim. 1:15 (*Today's English Version*)

WILL THE REAL PAUL MARTIN— STAND UP?

A high school friend of mine in Orange, California, said, "Man, when you drove up, my friends almost split [ran away], for with that white car, they thought you were a narcotics agent."

A waitress came up to me in Brinks' Cafe in Dallas, Texas, and said, "I get nervous waiting on you for you look so much like my doctor!"

I even got pinched on the back by the wife of a friend, thinking I was her husband.

My brother, Ted Martin, was teasing me publicly in a camp meeting, telling the crowd of the "troubles of Brother Paul." One of the older men of the crowd thought he was talking about Paul of the Bible and protested.

Let's go again from the ridiculous to serious reflection. I really pray that someone will say:

He talks kindly, like Jesus. He labors patiently, like Jesus.
He suffers misunderstanding, like Jesus. He gives himself.

No one will say anything like this, perhaps, but I can try to be such a person. I can enjoy trying to be like Him. And He helps those who try.

TAKE THIS WITH YOU:

*For me, 'twas not the truth you taught: to you so clear, to
me so dim,
But when you came to me, you brought a sense of Him!
And from your eyes He beckons me, and from your lips His
love is shed
Till I lose sight of you, and see the Christ instead.*
—Source Unknown

I know my critics say, "His letters are
impressive and moving but his actual presence
is feeble and his speaking beneath contempt."
—II Cor. 10:9-10 (Phillips)

FAIRLY RELIABLE JOE

That is exactly what the sign on his used-car lot says: "Fairly Reliable Joe." I like that. How foolish to advertise as "Perfectly Reliable"! No one has perfect judgment, perfect memory, perfect action. Good religion does not mean we never make mistakes, falter, fail. Even the wholly dedicated life has limited judgment, faulty information, and less than a perfect body.

Now, when the new Christian surrenders all to the Spirit of God, his heart is cleansed of its selfish spirit, strengthened, and lifted. Now we have a firm foundation. We are truly "fairly reliable." We have better direction by the Spirit. We are more careful to remember our weaknesses, and hold fast to Him. When we know we have been wrong, we quickly make the matter right!

With the same lack of judgment, the same poor memory, and imperfect strength, we are more "reliable" through the Spirit.

I can do business with "Fairly Reliable Joe." Most of the time his judgment is good. His heart's right. If something turns out about the deal that I did not see or if I cannot keep the promises I made, we can get together. For in the matter of the heart, we are very dependable.

If the above sounds confusing to you, you are fairly normal!

ANOTHER THOUGHT FOR ANOTHER DAY:

"That which binds lives together is always nobler
than that which divides lives apart."
—*Brooklyn Daily Eagle* (1908)

But ye shall receive power, after
that the Holy Ghost is come upon you.
—Acts 1:8

IT WAS IMPORTANT TO THEM—
IS IT TO YOU?

What was the main concern of Jesus for the disciples? Hear Him: "And, behold, I send the promise of my Father upon you: but tarry ye in the city of Jerusalem, until ye be endued with power from on high" (Luke 24:49). "And I will pray the Father, and he shall give you another Comforter, that he may abide with you for ever" (John 14:16). It was Christ's great concern that the disciples tarry . . . wait till the Holy Spirit came in this special way.

What was the main concern of the early church for the new converts? The eighth chapter of Acts tells of a good revival in Samaria. Phillip was the evangelist. Many were saved. When the apostles in Jerusalem heard of it, they sent Peter and John to Samaria. And here's what the Bible says about their coming: "Who, when they were come down, prayed for them, that they might receive the Holy Ghost: (for as yet he was fallen upon none of them: only they were baptized in the name of the Lord Jesus)" (Acts 8:15-16).

Paul urged all Christians to be Spirit-filled. He was Spirit-filled. He urged them to be sure about this. "For this is the will of God, even your sanctification" (I Thess. 3:10).

Let it be your concern too. The Spirit will come, cleanse, give strength and guidance. Open your heart wide to him.

A THOUGHT FOR TODAY:

Perhaps if we believed and received as the apostles believed and received the Holy Spirit, we would achieve as they achieved!

27

But when the Spirit of truth comes,
he will lead you into all the truth. . . .
He will give me glory, for he will take
what I have to say and tell it to you.
—I John 16:13-14 (*Today's English Version*)

LIFE AND THE SPIRIT

Life with Jesus was full and exciting, and He promised it would be even more so with the Spirit!

Life in the Spirit is more, much more, than a one-night experience, much more than a great feeling. It is a life . . . a way of life!

Life in the Spirit is being "in Christ." What does this mean? The favorite phrase of the apostle Paul is *"en Christos"* (Greek) "in Christ." It is being fully surrendered to Christ . . . all Christ's . . . not our own.

Life in the Spirit is Christ in us.

When the Spirit comes, He makes Christ very real to us. When the Spirit comes, He is Christ coming in.

Life in the Spirit is life directed by the Spirit. It is the Spirit of love which reproves, corrects and disciplines, guides, encourages, heals, and forgives.

Listen to the Bible tell of life in the Spirit; "Love must be completely sincere. Hate what is evil, hold on to what is good. Love one another as brothers in Christ, and be eager to show respect for one another. Work hard, and do not be lazy . . . . share your belongings . . . open your home to strangers" (Rom. 12:9-13, *Today's English Version*).

LET'S HEAR THIS:

Give me a faithful heart,
Likeness to Thee,
That each departing day
Henceforth may see

Some work of love begun,
Some deed of kindness done,
Some wand'rer sought and won,
Something for Thee."

—S. D. Phelps

Tarry ye in the city of Jerusalem, until
ye be endued with power from on high.
—Luke 24:49

WE ARE THERE

It is called the "Miracle of Pentecost" . . . a magnificent painting, 20 feet high, 124 feet long. Torger Thompson wanted to put on canvas the birthday of the Church, the Day of Pentecost. The figures are life-size. The moment is when the Holy Spirit came upon the 120 who had tarried in the upper room.

The painting is housed in a temporary warehouse in Dallas, Texas, until a permanent chapel is built. While we were viewing it, Mr. Thompson pointed to a praying figure, a Palestinian in the crowd, and yes, it was the artist. He had put himself into the picture.

We are there too, all of us who believe in the Holy Spirit. He is God's agent, making Jesus real to us.

We are there, we who love His Church. For this is the true birthday of the Church. Without the coming of the Holy Spirit, there would be no Church. That is why Jesus was so concerned that the disciples wait for the Spirit's coming. Today the true Church is made up of people who are Spirit-cleansed, Spirit-filled, and Spirit-led.

We are there. For we must wait for the promise of the Father too. It is for all who love Christ.

A SONG THAT ALMOST SINGS ITSELF:

Oh, to be like Thee! while I am pleading,
Pour out Thy Spirit, fill with Thy love.

My heart is fixed, O God, my heart is
fixed: I will sing and give praise.
—Ps. 57:7

A FIXED HEART

With Dr. James Strong's big, fat *Exhaustive Concordance of the Bible* on my big, fat lap, I can be a scholar, for it not only lists every word, every time it is used in the Bible, but it also gives a dictionary meaning of the original Hebrew and Greek words as well as their English meaning. (Don't tell anyone. Let them think I am a scholar.) Here is how it works:

"My heart is fixed." The word "fixed" is *kuwn* (using the English alphabet) pronounced *koon*. It means basically, "to stand erect." It also can mean "prepared, ready, perfect, stable, fixed."

OK; then let's make the outline. The psalmist says, and let us say:

1. My heart is *erect* . . . stands tall above the petty, foolish, little things that beg for time, for attention. I must put things in their order.

2. My heart is *prepared, ready.* The Spirit comes to open hearts . . . wide open. Let us prepare the way of the Lord. Every believer needs the fullness of the Spirit. And the Spirit comes to prepared, open hearts.

3. My heart is *fixed* . . . is locked on . . . to do His will. I am determined. I shall not wander from His course.

Also, the psalmist suggests that a fixed heart will be thrown into difficult places like, "My soul is among lions." Under those circumstances a fixed heart will cry unto the Lord . . . it will trust in God: "In the shadow of thy wings will I make my refuge until the calamities are past."

MY PRAYER FOR TODAY:

Dear God, may the radar of Thy Spirit guide me carefully today and lead me home.

Brethren, if a man be overtaken in a
fault, ye which are spiritual, restore such an
one in the spirit of meekness; considering
thyself, lest thou also be tempted.
—Gal. 6:1

LOVE-WATCHERS

"OK, weight-watchers will come to order. My, you look great! I notice you have only two chins now, Mrs. Tubbyhead. And Miss Creme Puffs, how much have you lost this month? . . . One half pound . . . good! Now we must keep our attendance up. For you get lots of help by hearing how others lose. Say, Mr. Sugar-tooth, I saw you slip into Dunk-Rite Doughnut Shop last night. What were you doing in there?"

Weight-watchers meet on Monday at 7 p.m.

Love-watchers meet on Wednesday at 7:30 p.m. For prayer meeting is for Love-watchers. Prayer meeting: where people far from perfect in judgment . . . tempted, set upon on all sides by the devil . . . people surrendered to God . . . Spirit-filled . . . get together to encourage each other, to pray for each other.

Love-watchers have this going for them: they know the real issue in the Christian life is love. They know the force of temptation, and they seek to share encouragement with others. They feel better, look better, are less spiritually tired as they lose their worries, fears, and religious fat.

OK, love-watchers, meet at 7:30 p.m. Wednesday.

A SONG TO SING TODAY:

> *He called me and He wooed me,*
> *And I am His today,*
> *As hand in hand we journey*
> *Along the Heav'nward way.*
> —Thoro Harris
> *Copyright 1954, 1962 by Lillenas Pub. Co.*

Follow peace with all men, and holiness,
without which no man shall see the Lord.
—Heb. 12:14

WE NEED THE SPIRIT

Every time I go down to Sather Gate at the south entrance of the University of California, where the "odd balls" congregate, I say, "We need the Spirit of God." The picture is of many seeking for something, for something real, for healing, for cleansing, for purpose. We, too, are searchers . . . after more of God. We need the Holy Spirit, in so many ways . . . the Spirit who cares, who calls, who convicts, who brings Christ in close.

In this twelfth chapter of Hebrews (read verses 13-16), we see three needs of the spirit:

We need the *healing* of the Spirit that our lame nature may be healed. "And make straight paths for your feet, lest that which is lame be turned out of the way; but let it rather be healed." A diseased spirit needs healing, a twisted affection needs healing.

We need the *sweetening* of the Spirit, "Lest any root of bitterness springing up trouble you, and thereby many be defiled." So much suffering is caused by sourness . . . lingering resentment . . . uncomfortable hatred.

We need the *discipline* of the Spirit, "Lest there be any [unclean] . . . person, as Esau, who for one morsel of meat sold his birthright." He was hungry. He wanted instant food. Loneliness is hard, clean living isn't easy. But Esau would have had all he wanted to eat, if he had just waited a little . . . kept his standing . . . kept his honor.

MAKE THIS YOUR PRAYER:

Holy Spirit, all divine, dwell within thie heart of mine;
Cast down every idol throne; reign supreme and reign alone.

—Andrew Reed

*I may give away everything I have, and
even give up my body to be burned, but if
I have not love, it does me no good.*
—I Cor. 13:8 (*Today's English Version*)

LOVE POEMS

Love is big right now! Love beads, love-ins, love songs, *Love Story,* and "Love gets it all together."

I said this jingle as a kid. Crazy, man!

> Love is a funny thing,
> Shaped like a lizard,
> Wraps itself around your heart,
> And nibbles at your gizzard.

Love does make you hungry. A lot of love is merely physical but true love is much more:

It is adjusting to others.

It is understanding, or trying to understand.

It is faithfulness . . . just standing by, being there—being right there—in sunny days and stormy.

It is reaching out to those who hold us off, who do not know our hearts.

It is open-mindedness, openheartedness.

These four lines have come to be some of the best known lines in the world, memorize them:

> He drew a circle that shut me out,
> Heretic, rebel, a thing to flout!
> But Love and I had the wit to win;
> We drew a circle that took him in.
> —Edwin Markham

Amen!

SOMEONE SAID THIS:

> *"Sympathy is two hearts tugging at one load."*

And all the tithe of the land, whether of the
seed of the land, or of the fruit of the tree,
is the Lord's: it is holy unto the Lord.
—Lev. 27:30

TITHING FROM A TO Z

A. All good and perfect gifts come from God. Why not return a tithe to Him? *B.* It helps the *budget* to tithe—yours and the church's. *C.* Tithing is God's plan for *church* financing. *D.* Tithing is a *duty* that is really a privilege. *E.* Tithing is a plan for *everyone. F.* Lay aside that 10 percent *first*—it's easier that way. *G. Give* and it shall be given unto you. *H. Happiness* is learning the tithing *habit. I.* Money can become an *idol;* tithing keeps it in place. *J. Jesus* said, "Where your treasure is, there will your heart be also." *K.* Tithing helps you *keep* the faith. *L. Love* and tithing go together; both are laws of God. *M.* Tithing is the life-support system of the *missionary. N.* "*No* good thing will he withhold from them that walk uprightly" (Ps. 84:11). *O.* Good givers give *offerings* with their tithe. *P.* Check your *purpose* in tithing: to succeed? No, to keep God first. *Q.* Ask faithful tithers if it is good business. A good *question. R.* "Wherein have we *robbed* thee? In tithes and offerings" (Mal. 3:10). *S.* It is *scriptural. T.* Tithing is giving *10 percent* of your income to God and the church. *U.* Tithing is a great plan for *you. V.* Other *victories* come too—when we win the battle of tithing. *W. Wait* patiently and see how tithing helps you and yours. *X.* When figuring your tithe, make few *exceptions! Y.* Begin to tithe early, while you're *young. Z.* "*Zero* in" on God's plan for you and your money.

A SONG TO GIVE HIM TODAY:

> *Give of your best to the Master;*
> *Give Him first place in your heart;*
> *Give Him first place in your service;*
> *Consecrate every part.*

Show a gentle attitude toward all.
The Lord is coming soon.
—Phil. 4:5 (*Today's English Version*).

CURL YOUR HAIR

"Jean's House of Gossip."

"Come in! Even if you don't want a permanent, the conversation in here will curl your hair."

"Put your mind into neutral, and let your tongue idle on."

"Through these doors pass some of the 'gossipiest' women in the world."

These are a few selections from my collection of "signs of the times."

Talk is so cheap, isn't it? But so valuable. To take time just to talk with a lonely old person is so worthwhile. To listen to a high school friend talk, talk, talk, will keep you in touch and give him strength. Witnessing for Christ usually means talking some.

I guess the devil knows the value of talking; that's why gossip and surmising and whispering are such a temptation.

There are no easy ways to stop gossip, but here are a few suggestions:

1. Practice thinking and saying something good about everyone whose name comes up in the conversation.

2. Search your own heart honestly for signs of jealousy and drive it out with the Spirit's help!

3. Keep close to those who seem "different" and perhaps unlovely to you. The closer you get, the better they look.

4. Pray daily for strength to treat others as you want to be treated.

LET'S SAY IT AGAIN:

"Let the words of my mouth, and the meditation of my heart be acceptable in thy sight, O Lord, my strength, and my redeemer" (Ps. 19:14).

*"Observe the sabbath day, to keep it holy,
as the Lord your God commanded you."*
—Deut. 5:12 (*RSV*)

NEVER ON THE LORD'S DAY!

Why is Sunday so special?

1. It is the Lord's Day, the Christian Sabbath, dedicated to God.

2. It should be a day of rest. It involves obedience to the fourth commandment. (There has been no repeal of the Ten Commandments.)

3. It should be a day of revival and reward. It is a time for very little everyday stuff and lots of God's business.

4. It is a reminder of God's place in our lives. Is He really Number One? A good day to practice it.

5. It tells of the Resurrection. The Early Church moved to the first day of the week from the Jewish seventh day, in joyful reminder of the resurrection of our Lord. It celebrated the release that God brought to Jesus and brings to our lives.

Make Sunday special!

1. Make it not a dull day, but special, different.... Less for self and more for God.

2. Be consistent! Help your TV set keep the Sabbath.

3. Make it a day of rest, renewal, and relaxation. Plan things that you don't do daily, nor even on vacation or Saturday.

4. Make it God's day. All days are His; all work is His—that is true. But other days are better, when the first day is for worship, praise, and prayer.

I WILL PRAY:

Lord, help me practice Your commandment, honor Your day, and so make other days better.

36

*I want men everywhere to pray, men who are
dedicated to God and can lift up their hands
in prayer without anger, or argument.*
—I Tim. 2:8 (*Today's English Version*)

JUST A FEW PRAYERS AWAY

Pastor Fred Wenger, a good friend of mine, wrote a little note on his Christmas card last year:

> "Remember there are some wonderful miracles, just a few prayers away."

What a lift this thought is!

It means that God is alive, real, active, and ready to help. He is able to break through into our mixed-up lives.

This good statement means, too, that God is ready but has given man a part in His plan. He can work without us but He chooses to give us a choice ... to plan and to work with Him ... or to try it without Him.

This line means that prayer is man's part ... to discipline his life, to show his real self, to make himself ready for God's touch.

I do not understand all that prayer means but I do know that I need to pray. I long to pray better, longer. Prayer does a lot for me. I can see more miracles that way and see them clearer.

Let's say it again: "There are some wonderful miracles, just a few prayers away."

Let us pray, keep praying, practice praying. Do it daily, on schedule and off schedule, in different ways ... but pray.

WHISPER THIS PRAYER:

*Teach me, dear Lord, to really pray in a self-forgetful way.
Teach me to trust; teach me to obey; to really pray.*

37

And as he was praying, the appearance of his countenance was altered, and his raiment became dazzling white.
—Luke 9:29 (*RSV*)

HE TURNED ON WITH THE SPIRIT

Jesus glowed. The disciples said that His face and clothes became dazzling white. Jesus (and I say it reverently) was really turned on!

We will never be turned on like this, but we can be aglow with the Spirit . . . turned on with Christ's love.

Be turned on in joyful song. A lot of screaming, chanting, and bad-mouthing are everywhere. So songs from a happy heart are good to hear.

Be turned on with praise! Praise the Lord! Amen! Hallelujah! These are great words. They encourage. They bless.

Be aglow with friendliness. "Do not neglect to show hospitality to strangers, for thereby some have entertained angels unawares" (Heb. 13:2, *RSV*).

Be aglow with prayer. Prayer gives to life a holy radiance. Patience, kindness, and peace come as we look upward.

Be aglow with love . . . His love, cleansing love, sharing love.

Jesus will be seen . . . for it is His Spirit that shines through us.

A SHORT STORY:

Jack pointed to the stained-glass windows where the apostles were pictured in the glass. "Who are they?" he asked. "Saints, Jack." "I see, Saints are people who let the light shine through!"

*Not that which goeth into the mouth
defileth a man; but that which cometh out
of the mouth, this defileth a man.*
—Matt. 15:11

THEY ARE A DIME A DOZEN

Have you been listening to bad talk ... swearing, crude stories? Does a "poor" word slip into your talk once in a while? Be different! There are rough-talking people everywhere. Be different!

Does it seem sort of smart to be sarcastic, disrespectful; to snarl, snap ... "put 'em down" ... parents, police, teachers ... those who are older or those who disagree? Be different. There are noisy second-guessers on busy corners ... and some even come to church.

Is it easy to treat your friends like con men? What can they give? Are your smiles real? Do you really want to be with them? Be different! There are "phonies" at every fellowship!

To cheat or to be honest! Is that the question? Is the eleventh commandment, "Thou shalt not be caught"? Be different! Be dependable! Be clean! Be courteous! Be real!

A fire-bomber threw his bomb into a store. The store burned, and the store next to that and the house next, and the next apartment on the corner ... but, you see, the bomber lived in the apartment and lost all he had too!

I WISH I HAD SAID THIS:

"This is the test of a gentleman: his respect for those who can be of no possible use to him."

We look not at the things which are seen,
but at the things which are not seen; for
the things which are seen are temporal; but
the things which are not seen are eternal.
—II Cor. 4:18

THINGS YOU CAN'T SEE

I am putting into this little book two favorite kite stories. Here's the first:

A boy was holding a kite which just went up into the low-hanging clouds. The kite was out of sight. The wind was steady but it was quite dark.

A man came by. "What are you doing?" he asked.

"Flying a kite."

"I don't see any kite . . . just string. What makes you think you're flying a kite?"

"Well, the clouds were not there awhile ago, and they will pass. And besides, I know it's there for I feel the pull in my hands!"

Now you make the application for yourself!

That is right. . . . Troubles will pass. It will be clear again, soon.

Yes, right. Things which may not be seen are still real. Things which we feel are important.

Quick answers are not always seen after prayer.

God's reasons for allowing sickness, even death, are not easily read or understood.

Rewards for good, honest living are not front-page news.

But God's Word and His Spirit pull us on.

TAKE THIS THOUGHT WITH YOU TODAY:

"God does not offer us a way out of the testings of life. He offers us a way through, and that makes all the difference."
W. T. Purkiser

Behold, I come quickly: blessed is he that keepeth
the sayings of the prophecy of this book.
—Rev. 22:7

SEND IT BACK

Jittery Joan, age five, finally found the Bible under the magazines and did not know what it was.

"What kind of a book is this, Mother?"

"It is God's Book."

"We had better send it back," Joan said thoughtfully.

"Why?"

"We aren't using it!"

God's Word, the Bible, needs use. It is for our use. It is full of helps for us. Don't ignore the best Book of all.

The Bible gets better with use. We learn to understand it. New things keep coming through.

The Bible is up-to-date. It really is. Times change and gadgets come and go, but people are not much different. So the Bible speaks to personal needs as modern as jet planes.

It is God's Book. God blesses the readers of His Book. So let's use it.

TODAY'S QUOTE:

"The more I read God's Word, the more I listen to it, the more I meditate upon it, the more I believe it."

—Wendell Wellman

*I know whom I have believed, and am persuaded
that He is able to keep that which I have
committed unto Him against that day.*
—II Tim. 1:12

THE UNKNOWN BUNDLE

Carrol was 16, blonde, blue-eyed. She was at the altar, and she "put the unknown bundle on the altar." What does that mean?

It was a phrase that was often used back there when Carrol was 16. It meant giving God your tomorrows . . . your life, for richer or poorer, in sickness and in health . . . like putting an unknown bundle in God's hands for good.

Now, I got to see what was in that unknown bundle. Carrol Chandler is years and years older now, but alert and alive to God. We have talked often of that big moment when she was 16, and of the many good, bad, happy, tragic, exciting, frightening days that have passed since then. Her college plans were delayed for a while, marriage to a young doctor, two children, happy times. Suddenly her son was killed! Then better times again: three more girls, her older girl in college—good days, hiking up the stream. Then the doctor died suddenly. The world fell in. Slowly, slowly, she fought her way up.

All the while, her heart was saying, "When I was sixteen, I put the 'unknown bundle' on the altar. It is still there!" And in each dark night, and happy day, the Lord was near.

I wished I had helped her more, for I married her daughter and I received so much more of love and understanding than I gave.

A BIBLE VERSE TO REMEMBER

Don't worry over anything whatever; tell God every detail of your needs in earnest and thankful prayer, and the peace of God, which transcends human understanding, will keep constant guard over your hearts and minds as they rest in Christ Jesus" (Phil. 4:6-7, Phillips).

*And it came to pass, that a whole year they
assembled themselves in the church, and
taught much people. And the disciples were
called Christians first in Antioch.*
—Acts 11:26

SUPERHICKS, PIGS, AND CHRISTIANS

Basketball in Indiana is "Hoosier Hysteria" and this year one of the four finalists were the "Superhicks" of Floyd Central High School of Southern Indiana. It is a country high school, comparatively small. The papers were calling them the "Hicks from Floyd County," but since they beat enough teams to be the state finalists, they were "Superhicks."

A lot of people call policemen, "Pigs." They used to call holiness people, "Holy Rollers." Even when the early believers were first called Christians, it was a bad name ... "You're a Christian, like that crazy One they crucified!"

It is the first step in propaganda, to give those who will not agree with you a label, a bad label—radical, worldly, Red, Nazi. You don't want to use their correct names ... you give them another ... a label ... so you can attack them.

It often happens that the labeled one lives so true, refuses to fight back, loves us in spite of our attack, until *their* way seems better. Their real purpose is seen, and our name for them becomes a good name.

Carry the name of Christ proudly.... Be a heads-up Christian!

A PRAYER FOR THE ASHAMED:

Dear Lord, the privilege of being called a Christian is such a precious privilege. Help me to carry the name carefully, hold it high, share it generously, love it dearly.

43

But God said unto him, Thou fool, this night
thy soul shall be required of thee: then whose
shall those things be, which thou hast provided?
—Luke 12:20

THREE BIG MISTAKES

A good many mistakes are soon forgotten—and should be. All of us make them . . . and most of the time we can fix things up and go on.

Yet some mistakes are costly, too costly. The Bible tells about a man who made three big mistakes. Read his story in Luke 12:16-21.

He had barns, cattle. He was proud of his great ability. He said, "I have more . . . will keep more. I have comfort, ease. I have all I need." But God had other ideas. "Tonight, you fool, you'll lose your life. Then what will happen to all of this?"

The man made three mistakes!

1. He mistook his body for his soul. He was thinking of all he could see, touch, hear, and feel, but the good life was more: love, worship, and soul business.

2. He mistook himself for God. God didn't matter. . . . He couldn't see Him . . . so he forgot Him. But God is very real. What a foolish mistake!

3. He mistook time for eternity, the big part of life. God has so much to give us . . . time here and there, too!

Mistakes like these are costly. Let's avoid them, even if it takes all we have!

A WORD TO REMEMBER:

> *For feelings come and feelings go,*
> *And feelings are deceiving,*
> *My warrant is the Word of God,*
> *Naught else is worth believing.*
> —Martin Luther

Those who seemed to be the leaders . . .
made no new suggestions to me.
—Gal. 2:6 (*Today's English Version*)

HEADLINES—TRUE OR FALSE

I get to noticing the headlines of the newspaper. Here's a sample, with the true story, telling what it is all about:

Not So Great White Hope: Is it a story of a white boxer to challenge Ali or Frazier? No, it is the weather forecast . . . not much chance of snow.

Youths Up in the Air over Science Project: Are a couple of boys having trouble with their project? No, Joe Harris and David Cubine have just built a hovercraft that skims along the ground on a cushion of air.

Plan Would Eliminate Two-Timing in State: Is there a law going through that keeps you from dating two girls at one time? No, a bill was discussed in the legislature to make Kentucky all Eastern or Central Standard Time.

Two Lusty Windbags Battle It Out over the South Atlantic: Is it the story of two camp meeting evangelists preaching at the Maryland Camp . . . like Rev. Ted Martin and I? Not really, it is the story of two hurricanes storming around in the Caribbean!

No, they are not always what they seem . . . these notices. . . . Nor can we turn from our course with every threat of trouble or storm. They usually are not as bad as they are made to appear. It seems to be a part of the business of the press and of the onlookers to make the problem bigger, or the hill higher, or the crowd noisier, or the man weaker than he really is.

Let's face things as they come. Do our best. Trust the results with God.

ANOTHER THOUGHT FOR THIS DAY:

Too often we seek a change of our condition, when what we need is a change of our attitude.

45

What gain has the worker from his toil?
—Eccles. 3:9, RSV

WHAT'S SO GOOD ABOUT FLYING?

I like to fly in 707s, 747s, 737s, DC-8s, DC-9s, Convairs, Pipers ... over the Andes, over the Alps, over South Bend, Indiana.

What's good about it?

Saves time ... but costs more than driving the car.

Convenient, saves energy ... but noisier than a bicycle.

Can go farther ... sometimes farther than you want ... to Cuba maybe.

Then every now and then questions like these pop into your head:

What are you doing with the time saved? Whom are you helping with the greater strength? Whom did you witness to right at home before you started on the trip to witness to those far away?

If I have saved time and strength, and gone a long way, I'd better work harder. For praying accomplishes more than flying. Fasting is good when I am powerless. Witnessing works at home too. A day is just so long; our strength is just so much ... and what we do for Christ is the only thing that lasts!

Besides, there are those who do not, and will not, fly: sick, hurt, stuck-where-they-are. They just have to stay, and stay, and stay. Now, the lessons of the good life will help. They learned to pray, to trust God, to have sympathy, to care, to share in the jet ... and it works on the ground.

There's Dallas ... Love Field ... flaps down, wheels down ... screech, rumble, whine, and whistle ... stop.

A GOOD THOUGHT FROM AN OLD BOOK:

"He does the most for God's great world, who does the best in his own little world."

And to you who are troubled rest with us,
when the Lord Jesus shall be revealed
from heaven with his mighty angels.
—II Thess. 1:7

NERVOUS IN THE SERVICE

Check these casual remarks that friends shared with me (and I wish they hadn't).

A psychiatrist was on his way to make a house call, carrying his couch, when he ran into an antique dealer carrying a grandfather clock. The doctor fell to the street from the impact, and yelled to the reeling antique man, "Why don't you wear a wristwatch like everybody else!"

Then there's the one about the neurotic coach who thought the football players in the huddle were talking about him.

And how about the nervous bank robber who blurted out "Don't stick with me, this is a mess up."

Or the enthusiastic young evangelist who hurried to the seeker at the altar and cried, "Stand on your hands and give me your foot and tell me you're going through."

Or the preacher who was so slow that when he took a tranquilizer it livened him up!

All right, so other people get nervous too! But I can work on this problem. Rest, medical attention, common sense, these help.

And there is trust . . . just simple trust in the Lord. "In all thy ways acknowledge him and he shall direct thy paths."

A SONG FOR THE NERVOUS:

Take time to be holy. Speak oft with thy Lord;
Abide in Him always, and feed on His word.
Make friends of God's children; help those who are weak,
Forgetting in nothing His blessing to seek.

—W. D. Longstaff

*Take heed that ye despise not one of these
little ones; for I say unto you, that in
heaven their angels do always behold the
face of my Father which is in heaven.*
—Matt. 18:10

IF I WERE AN APE OR AN ANGEL

Someone told me this dumb story: A friend phoned Horace one day and said, "Your wife just ran away with an orangutan (ape)." Horace seemed less shocked than expected, and answered quietly, "Well, that's all right. Guess I shouldn't have married an orangutan in the first place."

I'm neither an ape, nor an angel, but if I were, there are some things that wouldn't bother me:

1. The Ten Commandments. Apes can't read them and angels don't need them.

2. What other people think. Apes do their "thing" naturally, and angels are up and away.

3. The demands of holy living. Apes are not supposed to be holy and angels were never anything else.

I'm somewhere between the two. The difference is: I can choose. And with choice there is risk; there is struggle; there is guilt; there is suffering; and there is forgiveness, and joy, and fellowship.

To be able to choose is a gift of God's love! Guard it wisely.

WE BORROWED THESE THOUGHTS:

> *One day there passed along the silent shore,
> While I my net was casting into the sea,
> A Man, who spoke as never man before;
> I followed Him. New life began in me.
> Mine was the boat, but His the voice;
> And His the call, yet mine the choice.*
> —Joseph Addington Richards

How much better is it to get wisdom
than gold! and to get understanding
rather to be chosen than silver!
—Prov. 16:16

DO WHAT WE CAN

"The weather doesn't look good. A big storm center is headed our way. So keep *one* eye on the barometer, *another* on the sky, and *another* on the TV screen for late reports." Just a minute! What do you think I am—some freak with three eyes?

"What we must have at this school, is young men who will keep their feet on the ground, their noses to the grindstone, their ears to the ground, their heads in the clouds, at the starting blocks, giving it all they have." Hold it just a little! I'm not a contortionist!

"Give us women who can cook, bake, sew, mow the lawn, get the groceries, have babies, feed them, wash them, diaper them, spank them, keep her husband happy, iron his shirts, shine his shoes, manage his money, and come straight home from work smiling." Cool it, Henry, I'm not superwoman.

We would certainly be done in if we tried to do everything that is expected of us. Do nothing, then? No, that's the answer of the drifter.

Let us do what we can, in God's way, in God's time. He does not expect more than we can do. Best of all, He is there to help us. Let's plan and pray and practice to do better the things we have to do and we will find ourselves doing well!

A PLEDGE TO TAKE THIS MORNING:

> *Do all the good you can,*
> *At all the times you can,*
> *To all the people you can,*
> *In all the places you can,*
> *In all the ways you can,*
> *As long as you can.*

Not slothful in business; fervent in spirit; serving the Lord.
—Rom. 12:11

THREE LESSONS FROM BIG BUSINESS

Fred J. Barch, board chairman of the General Electric Company, answered some questions about big business and how to run it. Three of his answers seemed to speak to me:

How far ahead is your company planning? "It looks as if our plans can be brought together now by 1980."

We get ourselves in such a mess, at times, by not planning very far ahead. Don't we? Good work demands good plans.

How do you personally manage such a giant? "The problem is organizing it into segments that people can *get their arms around.*"

So in your little job and mine, nothing works like the personal touch.

Do you feel that an executive has to be a courageous man? "The time to go into things is when everybody else is getting out."

Stay right in there. Keep busy in your church; keep pulling for the Lord. A good time to show your love for Christ and the church is when some are coasting.

How do you spot a man you think will be useful in your business? "We go after him early, young. We expect men in their late thirties to be in responsibilities worth 50 million dollars."

Oh, oh! we had better not waste more time. Ours is really big business.

A PRAYER:

God give us men! A time like this demands strong minds, great hearts, true faith, and hands. God give us men.

Be ye kind one to another, tenderhearted,
forgiving one another, even as God for
Christ's sake hath forgiven you.
—Eph. 4:32

WILL YOU GET DOWN?

In an old book, I read a good story: Two boys, one bigger than the other, started across an ice-covered lake. They walked slowly, testing the ice. Soon they came to a break in the ice. The bigger boy could easily leap across the gap, or even step across. The little chap couldn't. It was doubtful, too, that the big one could step across carrying the little one because the edges were so slippery. Finally the "Big Guy" got an idea. Lying down across the gap, he made a bridge over which the "Little Guy" crawled.

We can bridge gaps for those around us too.

How about the gap of strangeness among those who visit our church for the first time? Take time to explain why we do things in certain ways—the different songs, the altar, the centered pulpit. Bend every effort to be extra friendly. Friendliness grows.

How about the gaps that failure and mistakes bring? Get down . . . bend . . . to where the defeated one is. Share one of your "flops" with him.

How about the gaps of age? Get down . . . bend if it breaks! Learn to know, to understand, to love the person, be he older or younger.

Don't forget this: Bending is good for losing spiritual "fat."

READ THIS NOW AND THEN:

> *Wherever you go, you will find the world's masses,*
> *Are ever divided into just two classes.*
> *And strangely enough you will find too, I've seen,*
> *There is only one lifter to twenty who lean.*

And the peace of God, which passeth all
understanding, shall keep your hearts
and minds through Christ Jesus.
—Phil. 4:7

SISTERS OF MISERY

Let's meet some sweetie-sweet sisters of Misery. Dr. W. T. Purkiser told of them in an editorial. I'll quote from him now and then (note quotation marks).

Meet *Miss Information.* She's everywhere. Pops up often. Dr. Wiley once said, "The problem is that so many people know so many things that aren't true." She's arrogant, this dumb sister. Our problem is that hasty actions based on careless research are always easier than carefully planned actions.

Meet *Miss Understanding.* She is a sad sister. Not having the facts, it is very easy to misunderstand. It probably started when we listened to Miss Information, who led us astray.

Close by here is another sick sister: *Miss Representation,* double cousin of the "Liars." She even lies by telling the truth ... one side of a situation ... "telling just part of the story as if it were the whole story."

"At the end of this sad and mischievous line is *Miss Behavior.*" What people think and feel is never so important as what they say and do.

"What-we-think and what-we-do may walk apart for awhile, but finally they join together."

So let's snub these sisters of misery: Miss Information, Miss Understanding, Miss Representation, Miss Behavior. So long, sisters.

A PRAYER FOR TODAY:

Keep us close to the truth, on the way, and alive unto God; for Thou art the Way, the Truth, and the Life.

52

Everyone that was in distress, and everyone
that was in debt, and everyone that was
discontented, gathered themselves unto him.
—I Sam. 22:2

UNCLE BUDDY

You'll hear this name sometime if you haven't already. You may see one of his books, *Pitchers of Cream, Sunshine and Smiles, The Story of Lazarus,* etc. You may even hear his voice on the record of his "Hospital Experience." I'm sure you'll hear some good preacher quote (or misquote) him. Uncle Buddy was a household word—still is in many places.

He is Rev. Bud Robinson, nationally famous evangelist . . . a really funny man but, more importantly, a great soul winner. . . . Lived and died working for his Lord.

Though poorly educated, he sent many to college.

Though afflicted a bit in speech, he spoke as loving and clear a message as any man of his time or since. And his heart was as big as the burden he carried.

He was born in the mountains of Tennessee; saved at a Texas camp meeting at age twenty; called to preach; and crisscrossed the world preaching the gospel. I was privileged to know him.

He made you laugh, really laugh; and slipped the truth to you while you smiled. He loved people and he loved the Lord.

Uncle Buddy was a living example of what God can do when a young man surrenders completely to the will of God. God used his quick wit, his deep commitment, his great heartbeat for all to bless thousands. Oh, for another Bud Robinson!

UNCLE BUDDY SAID:

"What is the description of a sanctified man? He has a level head, a sweet spirit, a big soul, a loving disposition, and a good heart."

53

*The steps of a good man are ordered by
the Lord: and he delighteth in his way.*
—Ps. 37:23

UNCLE BUDDY SAID—

"If the Lord is your Shepherd, then you are the Lord's sheep, and He has a perfect right to shear you any time He needs wool, and you have no right to bleat."

"A friend came to me not long since and said, 'Brother Bud, my religious joy has all leaked out. What is the trouble?' 'You keep your mouth open all the time,' I said, 'Thank you, Sir,' she said. 'You are welcome,' I said."

The blessing of sanctification will not keep you from snoring in your sleep, but, bless the Lord, it will cause you to wake up in good humor."

"It is Christlike to see something in the other fellow that is better than the things you see in your own self."

"Four things are needful to understand the Scriptures: First, Find out who is doing the talking. Second, Who he is talking to. Third, What he is talking about. Fourth, Believe he meant just what he said."

"There are sixty-six books in the Bible, 1,189 chapters, 31,173 verses, 773,746 words, 3,566,480 letters; and every book, chapter, verse, word, and letter is an index finger pointing to the Christ of Prophecy, the Christ of Bethlehem, the Christ of Calvary and, thank God, the Christ that walked off from Mount Olivet on the clouds saying, 'Good-bye, boys, I am going to prepare a place for you, and if I go and prepare a place for you I will come again and receive you unto myself.' "

AND WE ANSWERED IN OUR HEART:

"Even so come, Lord Jesus."

Heaven and earth shall pass away:
but my words shall not pass away.
—Mark 13:31

STUFF FOR BUMPER STICKERS, BULLETIN BOARDS, AND DORM WALLS

1. Largeness of heart is a Christian vitue. Is anything better?
2. Life on a fraction? Jesus came to impart life to the full.
3. Always put off until tomorrow what you shouldn't do at all.
4. Ignorance causes a lot of interesting arguments.
5. In God's will is our peace.
6. An airplane on the ground is safe, but planes were made to fly.
7. Let us laugh. It is the cheapest luxury man enjoys.
8. The great use of life is to spend it for something that outlasts it.
9. The man who removes mountains begins by carrying away small stones.
10. To make a long story short, don't tell it.
11. Christ wants players, not spectators.
12. No person can fully pay his debt to God, but he can make payments.
13. Some people are willing to serve God, but only as a consultant.

O.K., get some cardboard and make a sign, and practice it. For the world has a funny idea that those who carry signs, use bumper stickers, and testify in church, practice what they preach.

A PRAYER FOR CONCERNED CHRISTIANS:

Dear Lord, we are the only Bible a troubled world will read. Help us be what we say we are and live as we say we do, so that they will see You in us.

Then was our mouth filled with laughter,
and our tongue with singing: then said
they among the heathen. The Lord hath
done great things for them.
—Ps. 126:2

LAUGH AT YOURSELF

It really happened. I told the same story two services in a row! I noticed the story didn't seem to have the same "punch" it had the night before. My wife looked startled. The pastor looked at her . . . with sympathy, I believe.

Oh, me! We were pretty low when we stopped by the home of some friends for a lunch after church. The man said, "Why not tell the story every service now?"

That's what I did! And it got so that at the end of the week when I would say, "Reminds me of a preacher who . . ." the crowd would burst into laughter.

I learned some things . . . again. Mistakes are made by many, and some of us make them often. I'm sure I can make fewer if I try. And the best way out is to laugh at myself, and to get others to laugh with me!

Laughter is a tonic for the body and soul. It is so much better, too, if the laughter is not directed toward anyone else!

A PRAYER FOR THIS DAY:

Dear Lord, as I get older, make me wiser, and help me to remember there is something to be gained from everything—even from my failures.

A good man brings good out of the
treasure of good things in his heart.
—Luke 6:45 (*Today's English Version*)

A PRAYER, WHEREVER YOU ARE

Dear Lord: They died last night! Not physically, but worse.

I saw them: fuzzy-cheeked kids, drunk, doped, slapping conformity in the face!

Why don't they think of tomorrow, Lord?

They cheated yesterday, Lord, married and phoney . . . cheap smiles . . . and glossy homes.

Why don't they think of tomorrow?

They ran away . . . split . . . heavy hearts. A bunch from nowhere going nowhere.

They weren't really afraid to face it, but they didn't . . . life is a monster . . . too big . . . run!

But, Lord, life is still here tomorrow.

They are listless, Lord. Dreams are out . . . brains blown.

And what of tomorrow?

Give me help, Lord, to love, to follow, to heal, to give . . . to give them Jesus.

He will be here . . . tomorrow!

A SHORT THOUGHT FOR A LONG DAY:

"A man's character is like a fence: it cannot be strengthened by just a coat of paint."

Let thine eyes look right on, and let thine
eyelids look straight before thee.
—Prov. 4:25

LOOK STRAIGHT

Do you like push-ups, jogging, early morning exercise? Here's a real hard one. It will take all the strength you have: Try looking right in the eyes of one who has some glaring deformity or scar.

I was standing in line at an airline ticket agency. The young man behind said something about the weather and as I turned, I saw the most scarred face I had ever seen . . . no regular features like nose, ears, a mouth. I can't describe it. It wasn't a face. Then I practiced the hard one. Looking him straight in the eyes. He was a soldier, fresh from a "million face graftings" and now on his way home! I felt like he wanted to practice using his new mouth and I wanted to practice looking him in the eyes.

There are other kinds of scars and deformities in the lives of those near us. They are all too aware of them! When they are with us they hope to forget their handicaps, their repaired lives. We can help them by just looking straight at their "todays," their hopes.

I want others to look at me like this. There is so much that looks strange. I thank God for His repair job . . . spiritual corrective surgery . . . for the healing of His love. But some scars remain. Thanks for looking straight ahead!

TAKE THIS FORMULA FOR HAPPINESS WITH YOU:

> *"A faith fit to live by,*
> *A self to live with,*
> *A purpose in life that is fit to live in"*

*The fruit of the righteous is a tree of
life; and he that winneth souls is wise.*
—Prov. 11:30

LIGHTNING DOES STRIKE TWICE

Johnson Frazee of Scottsdale, Arizona, and his son Ernie are partners in business, and partners in another business too—witnessing for Christ. And this is big business. Here's their story:

Johnson Frazee has found a real ministry in picking up young hitchhikers around Phoenix, Ariz., as he goes and comes in his work. He quickly turns the conversation to the Lord. Now Ernie has started to do the same. One evening Ernie picked up Mike Johnson, took him home, telling him all the way of the love of Christ and the wonderful privileges of grace.

About ten days later, imagine Mike's surprise when, "hitching" again, he was picked up by Ernie's dad, Johnson Frazee ... another of God's coincidences. Mr. Frazee drove him home, too, all the while telling of the Lord, and stopping to pray with him. Then Mike admitted that "another guy had given him the same 'business' ten days before."

Johnson Frazee invited Mike to his home, ... told him to let them know when he could come. Mike phoned a day or so later. Ernie picked him up and, that day, Mike found the Savior. Though Satan has bounced him around a lot, Mike is gaining spiritual strength daily. I met him in days of revival a few months later. He's witnessing of a great way of life that he has found to be abundantly satisfying.

TAKE THIS THOUGHT WITH YOU:

"I don't know any other way than to witness with love."
—*Johnson Frazee*

But now he is dead, wherefore should I fast?
Can I bring him back again? I shall go
to him, but he shall not return to me.
—II Sam. 12:23

MY FRIEND—GONE

What do you do when you lose your best friend? That happened last Thursday. He died the way he lived...in the service of the Lord, sitting with friends...a moment of silence ...death...heaven.

What do you do? You cherish every memory! You laugh again at those fun times. You reflect again on the long, hard pull together. But you can't go back.

What do you do? You plan to meet again. There will be reunion in heaven. Not an idle dream, nor wishful thinking, for to all of us Jesus said, "Where I am, you will be also." So my resolve to go to heaven is that much stronger.

What do you do? You stop awhile and look at yourself. For death is certain...no one will escape. You can't imagine how it will feel, but you can be ready. My friend, Whit, was so alive, so busy, so involved in the Master's work. He was ready. There was no need for late "cramming for the final." Just live right and you will die right.

What do you do, when you lose a friend? You just work a little harder. My friend did so much good. Maybe I can pick up a loose cord he dropped and do it for him and do my own things better! I can love people more...be friendly to all...say an encouraging word to everyone. And I can look forward to talking it over with him when we meet again.

ANOTHER SONG TO SING:

> *When I walk through that dark, lonesome valley,*
> *My Savior will walk with me there.*
> *And safely His great hand will lead me*
> *To the mansions He's gone to prepare.*

Listen to this secret: we shall not all
die, but in an instant we shall be changed,
as quickly as the blinking of an eye,
when the last trumpet sounds.
—I Cor. 15:51-52 (*Today's English Version*)

DOES JESUS KNOW WE ARE COMING?

She couldn't have been more than six years of age, this girl from Omaha, and she was in New York City for the first time. She was riding up in an elevator in the Empire State building . . . somewhere around seventieth floor . . . She said anxiously to her father, "Daddy, does Jesus know we are coming?"

Yes, He does . . . and He is preparing a place for us. "I go to prepare a place for you. And if I go . . . I will come again, and receive you unto myself; that where I am, there ye may be also." Death is not all. There is so much of real living to do . . . in heaven . . . where He is.

The change between here and there may be sudden . . . and frightening to think of . . . but it will be a change . . . a tremendous change. It will happen when Jesus returns. He promised to return . . . and things look more like it now than ever. It would be no surprise to many if Jesus came today. It will happen when death comes . . . this too is certain. It happens every minute. It will be close to all of us this year, one way or another.

No, I can't just sit around and worry about it. I can be on my way . . . on my way to heaven . . . forgiven . . . Spirit-blessed, telling of His love . . . urging others to come. . . . For Jesus knows we are coming . . . and He is ready.

LET'S SING AGAIN:

> *When we've been there ten thousand years,*
> *Bright, shining as the sun,*
> *We've no less days to sing God's praise*
> *Than when we first begun.*

We are troubled on every side, yet not distressed;
we are perplexed, but not in despair.
—II Cor. 4:8

GO FLY A KITE

Here's the second kite story. Suppose kites could talk:

"Man, look, they have me all tied up. Look at that long string and that crazy tail they've tied on to me."

"Man, if I could get loose, split, shake this scene."

"Man, we'd soar . . . move . . . go."

No. Without the crazy tail, the kite would zigzag, uncontrolled. Without the string, the kite would fall.

Restraints, like leashes, are troublesome . . . kids irritated by parental restrain . . . young couples galled by family training . . . some questioning the standards of the church.

Wouldn't it be great if life could promise us, like the manufacturers do, "Five years of trouble-free use"?

The demands of preparation, school, practice. . . . Why all this time in school?

So, pulling aginst the strong winds of adversity;

Against the tricky winds of impatience;

Against the passing whims of "big deals";

Against the returning streams of temptation;

Tied to principles of love, promises that are eternal, relationships that are precious.

This gives life a lift!

A GOOD QUOTE BY A GOOD MAN:

"Soft nests are for little birds, and whatever God wants His children to be, it is not that they be little."

—W. T. Purkiser

We hanged our harps upon the willows in the midst thereof.
—Ps. 137:2

IT SHALL RING AGAIN

In front of the Cadet Chapel of the United States Air Force Academy in Colorado Springs, Colo., there is a bell . . . a silent bell, for its clapper was immobilized. It would not ring again until the prisoners of war were freed. The bell was cast in the war area, flown here, and set up by friends and buddies of these prisoners. The enemy wouldn't say much about the prisoners, and word leaked out that the boys were being treated poorly. So it was a glad day when the prisoners came home.

And there is rejoicing in heaven, when one sinner repents. No song or music is as good to hear as the song of a sinner set free.

Yes, and what of the ringing of the bells of peace! Oh, that men would war no more! Why should brother hate brother and friend lose friend?

O friend, there will be another day of glad reunion when from the ends of the earth God's own shall gather in His land, in eternal peace.

Jesus promised. It will be as He promised.

A PRAYER FOR TODAY:

Dear Lord, give us peace, Thine own sweet peace, we pray. And keep us near Thee till the morn shall brighten and the mists of sorrow and sighing flee away.

For this God is our God for ever and ever:
he will be our guide even unto death.
—Ps. 48:14

VOICES THAT ARE HUSHED

In the book, *Get Up and Go,* I closed with three articles about death. A mother told me recently that as she read them she questioned (and rightly so) why such thoughts should be in a book for the young. Then, believe it or not, her daughter suddenly died at twenty-one years of age. And among her effects, the little book was found in which several lines of these articles were underlined. Her mother thanked me for those serious thoughts.

It is true . . . all voices shall be hushed. In the Memorial Church at Harvard University, there hangs a bell, cast in England, bearing the inscription, "In Memory of Voices That Are Hushed."

Some voices are young when they are hushed, never getting a chance to sing their big song. A bright future beckoned and that was all.

Then you who read these words and I who write them must use our voices well . . . must make these hours and days count.

In the same church at Harvard there is a sculpture, "The Sacrifice" by Malvina Hoffman. It is a fallen knight, young, strong, with a sorrowing figure at his head.

Let us, too, if we must fall, be sure that we fall in the fight for right, in the labor of love for souls. For life is found when it is spent in really caring!

TAKE THIS THOUGHT WITH YOU:

> *They might not need me, yet they might.*
> *I'll let my heart be just in sight.*
> *A smile so small as mine might be*
> *Precisely their necessity.*
>
> —Emily Dickinson